Wild Boy

To Margo
with love

Wild Boy

WHAT I WANT TO TELL YOU

John Du Cane

ISBN: 1546449655
ISBN 13: 9781546449652
Library of Congress Control Number: 2017907500
CreateSpace Independent Publishing Platform
North Charleston, South Carolina

WILD BOY
WHAT I WANT TO TELL YOU

Why do we tell each other the stories we do, about ourselves?

What are we trying to say about who we are?

And why do we repeat the same set of stories over and over and over?

What makes a memory live on, at the expense of all other possible memories?

These here are those stories of mine that I have chosen over the years to pluck from the shards of my past—and repeat. These pieces now polished up—to be placed against the black velvet of my full and hidden history...

In each, I am wanting to tell you something about myself. Strung together, the pieces form a pattern—to paint a certain portrait of the self as it wants to be seen.

What singular event seems to vibrate with particular meaning for the teller—and what makes the audience respond with pleasure to the tales so told?

If the listener responds to the teller's tale, he does so out of sympathetic resonance. Some chord that strikes a note of recognition or reflection. So, once told—when received—the tale is no longer about me. It is about you...

Table of Contents

CHAPTER 1

Playing with Fire

I'm Gonna Burn Your Bush

In Sierra Leone, the elephant grass turns to parchment in the bleached heat of the dry season. Eight-foot columns of tinder waiting for a friendly match…

Down by the reservoir, my brother and I would run wild looking for toads to spear, lizards to shoot, snakes to chase, birds to startle, ant columns to kick, butterflies to net—while the hawks circled and spied in the bright blue sky.

Not much beats the excitement of running pell-mell through the crackling, bursting grass when it rages up—whipped by the wind—into a galloping roar of sparks and flame. Fun as good as sex, at least for a kid.

Who knows whether we ever really jump-started a bush fire or two—just for the hell of it? I like to think so. I do know, for sure, we loved to play in that burning bush…

Fun too, were the kill-parties in the clearings beyond the grass. When the fire jumped forward, every hidden critter had to dash for safety—or be roasted alive.

But on the perimeter lurked machete-wielding, stick-poised villagers, looking to stock their dinner pots…

Every kind of crawling, wriggling creature would pour out from the edges of the fire, to be met with cries of exultation, the thump-thump of blades and staffs slicing and raining down on them.

Few would escape.

And those few would most likely find themselves suddenly skewered in the claws of a hawk, soon high in the sky and squirming in their final, bug-eyed moments.

A giant iguana to my young eyes once belted out in all its multi-colored magnificence, to meet a majestic death in a circle of flashing knives. This I found wrenching—and paused me in my delight.

Your Car's on Fire

The Buick Century belched to a stop on red. Fairview and University, in a scarred section of St. Paul. Gray, squat blocks, gray road, gray sky. A lousy nothing of a day.

The boat-sized beater's peeled and washed-out greenish paint job fit right in: drab-on-drab.

Easy Does It cautioned the sticker on the rear. Don't think too hard, don't think too much at all…

She honked.

Head fixed forward, my eyes slid to the right. I didn't take in the color, make and model that revved beside me. Sagging skin, distressed blonde hair, bright red lips—the lady was mouthing and waving at me.

I twisted over and cranked down the window. Gust of sharp cold. And an oily, smoky stench…

"Excuse me," she yelled, "did ya know your car's on fire?"

I craned by neck over the door—fatty tongues of dirty yellow licked up at me from below.

"No, I didn't ma'am. Thank you."

Her eyes hardened, she hesitated, shook her head and accelerated out of my life.

I leapt out and yanked open the hood. The oil cap was missing-in-action. A black slick had spilled across the cowling. And at some point, the oil had just lit itself up.

Perhaps fortunately, the flames flickered out while I stood there watching and wondering…

Robert Fulghum told a story about firefighters who rescued a man from a burning bed. As the firefighters heaved him off the mattress, he remarked, "It was on fire when I lay down on it."

Myself, I have lain down—just way too many times—on burning beds. But a burning car? Just this once.

From Toys to Tar

There's a special magic as a child to setting fire to things you love.

Squatting on the garage concrete at four years old, I watched in fascination as my plastic truck went up in smoke. From a garish paint job to a syrupy, black tar that oozed into a satisfying puddle…

My reverie was pierced by my brother's cries: "Mummy, Mummy, Richie's burning his toys!"

A mother's fear and rage in the sands of the Kalahari…

Dad showed up in the late afternoon from his shift in the diamond mine.

"Beat him, John! Beat him!" was the greeting from my mom.

All Dad really wanted when he got home was an affectionate hug and a stiff whiskey—not some ritualized child abuse…

I sensed his reluctance—which mitigated some of the pain—as he broke a couple of rulers on my little white butt…

BURNING DOWN THE HUT

Winchester, England. Pre-prep school days. Seven years old. The landlady Fleurette had a garden hut in her back yard. I loved the smell of soil and rotting vegetation mixed with the metallic scent of tools and a beat-up lawnmower.

Jammed against the back was a broke-down desk full of seed packets, newspaper clippings, gloves, boxes of matches and other junk.

Now, this all would make for a pretty good blaze....

I got things going and skedaddled as the flames took hold. Shortly after, billows of black smoke started to pour from the hut's door—accompanied by screams of alarm from the alerted landlady.

Fleurette quizzed me. I denied everything—despite my obvious guilt.

Upstairs after the interview, I got my just reward—writhing around on the carpet, shielding myself from the blows and furious shrieks of my dear mother.

We had been due to go on an excursion to the Tower of London, to see the Black Prince's armor, the dungeons and the torture devices... Not any more.

CHAPTER 2

Brushes with Greatness

PIERCE MY NIPPLE

PETER BLOCH OF 24 FRAMES distributed my films in the early seventies—and I sometimes reviewed his various underground offerings for *Time Out* magazine. One evening in '71, Peter spooled out a stateside piece called ***Robert Having His Nipple Pierced***.

About 45 minutes—shot in a white-on-white, high-ceilinged room, with Andy Warhol silver pillows floating up and down. Front and center, a half-naked gentleman, propped in the arms of his lover. Some balding, pretend doctor ham-fistedly pierces the young man's left nipple. A bottle of booze is passed backwards and forwards. A hypnotic voice lays down a compelling monologue of reminiscences, anxieties and literary raves.

The movie was cool in its one-stare Warhol way, but it was the relentless monologue that grabbed me by the balls and wouldn't let go. My biggest take away: I got to hear about the flamboyant French writer **Blaise Cendrars**—whom the narrator had been so inspired by.

I was heading to the States for July and August, so Peter suggested I look up the movie's director **Sandy Daley**, in New York. Sandy lived on the tenth floor of Hotel Chelsea.

Sandy and I hit it off and she invited me to stay. But no sex. She was recovering from hepatitis. I would have rammed on in regardless, but Sandy was not about to share her egg-yolk eyes and banged-up liver with my reckless desire.

Every day the movie's voice, **Patti Smith** and the movie's nipple man, **Robert Mapplethorpe** would swing by. Patti was always so serious. Never saw her cut a smile. Hip coolness reigned. I didn't connect with her much. In hindsight, I should have thanked her for turning me on to Blaise Cendrars. That might have opened the gates a little.

Later, I reviewed the film for *Time Out* and arranged for a photo of her to be placed on the front cover. A famous shot in the end—a half-naked Patti swinging a hammer. Got a friendly note from her after that: "Hey, thanks for splashing my tits all over your magazine."

Robert was a sweetie. Attentive, kind, solicitous... One day he suggested I walk down the block to his loft—so he could show me his artwork. His pieces inserted themselves into my brain. On entering his passageway, a very well-photographed, carefully-composed shot of four male buttholes said hello. The second art piece was a pair of men's briefs stretched tightly on a small white canvas. I made some cool, hip, appreciative noises and the rest is a blur...

Before Her Murder

I met the precocious and ever-mischievous **Julian Allason** at Aix-en-Provence, where we were both pretending to study French literature and philosophy. Julian wangled press passes for both of us from the ***Daily Express*** to the Cannes Film Festival in May 1968.

A nice intro: watching the Cannes screening of *Yellow Submarine,* with all four of the **Beatles** sitting in the row behind us...

The highlight: Julian photographing **Roman Polanski** with **Sharon Tate** in his hotel room...

Roman quickly dispensed with the two teenagers and began jabbering away on the phone, in three languages.

The beautiful and ethereal Sharon Tate led us out onto the balcony overlooking the beach. We discussed astrology and related New Age subject matter in a dreamy kind of way...

Just 13 months later, members of the **Charlie Manson** gang butchered the heavily-pregnant Tate. To draw a line from the Cannes balcony visit, to her grisly end in Hollywood, takes a wrenching stroke of the pen.

Our Cannes Film Festival shenanigans ended abruptly just a few days later, when **Jean-Luc Godard, Francois Truffaut** and **Claude Lelouch** successfully agitated to have the event shut down, in solidarity with the revolting workers and student protesters.

I had lunch that winter in London with Julian, his mom and his younger brother **Rupert Allason**. Rupert later became a military historian, a Conservative MP and the author of numerous books on espionage, under the pen name **Nigel West**. A smiling brightness and effervescent wit is how I remember both of them…

Want Some Cocaine?

Donald Cammell and **Nicolas Roeg** made the cult film, *Performance*, starring **Mick Jagger, James Fox** and **Anita Pallenberg**. In 1970, I interviewed Donald for *Time Out*—the beginning of an intense connection that flared and finally fizzled after six or so months.

One day, Donald invited me to an event. Turned out to be **Keith Richards'** birthday party at Olympic Studios. The Stones were jamming away at *Sticky Fingers* with friends like **Eric Clapton**. **George Harrison** floated around looking majestic, while London's gilded youth circled each other with cool nonchalance.

A long trestle table sagged under some fine treats—including plates of dark chocolate hash cookies. I munched on a few…

Later, dazed and buzzed, I wandered back toward the recording booth. Donald was lying on the floor with an amused lady staring up at me—**Bianca Jagger**. She extended a hand… "Want some cocaine, John?" First person who had ever offered me uptown… I was off to a good start.

My ride enhanced, I headed into the booth itself, sat down on the couch and listened to the wall of sticky-fingered sound. I felt a hip touch mine. It was Mr. Mick, in to listen too. He gave me his beatific, big-lipped smile and we sat back together for a while as the music washed over us.

MASTER LOU

As a 19-year old undergraduate at Cambridge, I picked up a copy of *The Velvet Underground and Nico*, followed by *White Light, White Heat.* These two albums celebrate drug addiction, polymorphous sexuality and every manner of deviant behavior. They also contain incandescent lyrics, a burning soulfulness and a brilliantly visceral music that is timeless in its impact. Wild to the bone... haunting, beautiful.

Not long after, the artist-in-residence at Kings College, Cambridge, **Mark Lancaster**, gave me a note of introduction to his friends **Ted Hughes** and **Andy Warhol**. Which led me to hanging out at the Factory and meeting **Lou Reed** at **Max's Kansas City**.

It was a tough time for Lou's band. One night it was just me and my girlfriend dancing in front of the band upstairs, with an impassive **Jonas Mekas** the sole audience.

40 years after we first met, Lou re-entered my life, through our mutual passion for Chen Tai Chi. Through a shared lineage, I met him at a Tai Chi seminar in New York, then on a short film project in St. Paul where Lou acted opposite my daughter, Nicole.

Legend has it, he died doing Tai Chi, with his eyes open, held by his wife, **Laurie Anderson**, a look of rapture on his face.

Cobra Blood and a Shot of Scotch

Sam Robards is an actor and a physical culturist. His dad was **Jason Robards**, his mum **Lauren Bacall**. Sam got certified as a kettlebell instructor and came to a flexibility workshop taught by myself, **Pavel** and **Steve Maxwell**.

Sam was cool. While eating at an Indian restaurant in Minneapolis we shared stories about the wildest things we'd ever eaten. Like wasps, baby scorpion and locusts.

Sam had a good story, but he was gun shy on the full reveal…

While filming in Thailand, he visited a street shack selling cobra blood. A certain A-list star was part of the party…

The young Thai server jammed a wriggling cobra onto a large nail stuck out from a dark-stained beam. Sliced the body open from the neck. Caught the gush of blood in a beer glass— then splashed in a generous shot of Scotch.

The movie star grabbed the glass and chugged the entire contents in a few gurgly gulps. There was a pause. Then:

"Gaaaaarrrggghhh!" He spewed the entire contents all over his mates at the table…

Sam absolutely refused to name the star.

Some years later, I was watching a formidable movie, *Collateral Damage*, based on the true story of a group of Marines abducting, raping and murdering a young Vietnamese villager. Suddenly—as a military pastor—up popped Sam.

And I had my answer. **Sean Penn.**

THE LATTER DAY LUNCH

In 1971, the obscure Canadian film maker **Kris Patterson** invited a group of high-ego types to sit around an open-air feast, sip champagne, drive rolled banknotes across mirrors caked with coke—and fire up an endless supply of hash-laden spliffs.

Twelve of us each pontificated for a few minutes in a deliberately self-important manner on a subject most dear to our self-involved hearts…

The most notable—and most understated—of the group was **Donovan**. Our over-the-top punkster posturing ground the gears of his gentle, flower-child spirit—and he took off to a corner of the lawn, to play guitar with his wife **Linda Lawrence**.

(Linda had previously been with **Brian Jones** and had had a kid, Julian with him…)

Kris spliced in clips of carnage from the streets of Belfast by way of ironic commentary. The result was **The Latter Day Lunch**—one of those bizarre shorts that crawl from the cutting room to a single showing and then disappear without trace.

Kris came to a grisly end—straight out of a **David Cronenberg** movie. His drunken head was bashed in at a motel by a beautiful, pill-popping psychopath. He had met the lady on an art counseling gig at a Canadian psychiatric hospital. Kris had wangled a weekend pass for her to accompany him to that rendezvous.

She fled the scene—and Kris lay there for several days before they found him…

ANGER RISING

While at Cambridge I became obsessed with underground cinema—even forming a film society to show early Warhol movies like *Chelsea Girls*—which required simultaneous projection of two reels side by side…

Tony Rayns was a fellow undergraduate and by far the most influential film critic of us all. Tony worshipped the homo-erotic shorts by **Kenneth Anger** and did his poor best to emulate them in his own film work. I respected Anger's work, but the black magic and the homo-eroticism were not for me.

However, after **Donald Cammell** introduced me to Anger in the late seventies, we shared some memorable moments. Donald's mother had been a close friend of **Aleister Crowley**—a major inspiration for Kenneth…

I got to watch *Lucifer Rising* and various works in progress at Anger's apartment. I will never forget the sight of **Marianne Faithful** smacked out of her gourd, slowly climbing up an absurdly steep Celtic stone stairway cut into a mountain. And then there was **Bobby Beausoleil**, the unapologetic Manson cohort and celebrity murderer…

The hip fascination with Devil worship seemed childish, naïve and mistaken, to my mind—which was more attuned to a Buddhist approach to life. But Anger had an endearing intensity about him that, for me, balanced out the mania.

ACID IN MY TEA

For a brief and gorgeous time, I went out with the supertalented and altogether-special **Penny Slinger**. Penny dripped sex. A mystical surrealist with a penchant for the sublimely erotic, she went on with **Nik Douglas** to produce the seminal *Sexual Secrets*—which helped initiate the modern Tantra movement.

I met the straight-laced parents at her art show. Mom and Dad looked politely pained. I think the wedding cake—with its engorged penises thrusting up from the white icing—might have set them off a little…

One of Penny's girlfriends asked, "So… the million-dollar question… did Penny use yours as the model?"

"I'm not that small…"

Just before we hooked up, Penny had acted in a histrionic, acid-laced shambles of a movie, ***The Other Side of the Underneath***, directed by **Jane Arden**. I found it truly repellent.

Over Christmas, Penny invited me to share an evening with Sally the sad-faced cellist from ***Underneath***…

In the kitchen, the ladies served me tea and we chatted idly about this and that. At some point the light began to bend and colors to bleed and swell… they had spiked my tea with acid… big time… shades of the movie…

I have never been a fan of threesomes—in any of the versions I've been involved in. I like deep intimacy and communion with one person. I've always found the dynamic of a third wheel to be awkward. The mega-hit of acid blurred some of the edges this time round—but still not my cuppa…

THE ANGRY DWARF FROM HORROR HOSPITAL

Have you ever had a character from a horror movie suddenly show up for real in front of you? I have. I blame **Antony Balch**.

1973, Tony invited me to a screening of his *Horror Hospital* which I reviewed with irreverence in *Time Out*. My favorite character in the movie was a bizarre dwarf, Frederick, hammed up to the hilt by **Skip Martin**. I forget my exact phrasing, but I used some wildish words to describe Skip's performance.

Shortly after the review hit, I was hunching over my Olivetti on the top floor office of *Time Out*, when I sensed a presence to my right…

The crazed dwarf from *Horror Hospital* stood before me, angry, waving his arms in front of my face. Skip pitched me a load, hammering my insensitivity to dwarf-people. My ill-considered choice of phrasing had come across as prejudice.

"Frederick" was kind enough not to slit my throat, as he had so happily done to the hippies in the hospital. I invited him for a drink at a nearby pub and he filled me in on his fascinating past, acting in everything from **Otto Preminger's** *Saint Joan* to **Roger Corman's** *The Masque of the Red Death*.

Tony died of stomach cancer at the age of 42. Besides *Horror Hospital* I owe him for having introduced me to

William Burroughs at his apartment on Duke Street. Tony had labored for years to get Bill's *Naked Lunch* turned into a movie, with **Mick Jagger** as the star. Fortunate, really, that the project foundered—so that later **David Cronenberg** could do it the justice it deserved.

CHAPTER 3

Past Lives, Present Lives

MEETING ADONIS AT THE CROSSROADS

JOHN SCHOFILL HAD BEEN A nuclear engineer, until he downed enough acid and became an underground filmmaker. I met John in Berkeley, on a summer vacation from Cambridge.

"John, you've got a very spiritual face—I'd like you to star as the Soul in my film on the **Tibetan Book of the Dead**." I think it helped that I had shoulder-length hair, a raggedy beard and a yellow Indian shirt with red mantras painted across it.

"Sure, Paul, when do we start?"

Paul and I road-tripped to the Four Corners region, where at one point I found myself spread-eagled buck naked hanging from a cliff at dawn, thinking "I don't remember this being part of the *Tibetan Book of the Dead*—and what in hell am I doing here?"

Done with the shoot, Paul dropped me on the edge of Berkeley and I hitched out a coupla hundred miles to a desert crossroads.

A lone figure stood with his thumb out. Damn! It was **Tony Meyers**. An actor friend of mine from Cambridge. Didn't even know the bugger was in the States…

Tony's clean-cut, Adonis profile and buff physique got us to New York in three days flat. He would do the thumbing—and I would lurk in the shadows. When the hopeful victim pulled up, I would scuttle from behind my rock and join the band.

Like writing on water, there is an indecipherable beauty to the mysteries of these spooky meetings. How can they be? It's as if there was an invisible network of souls seeking each other out again and again—to reconnect and rework past karma.

Do You Have a Sister—And Is Your Dad a Butcher?

In Istanbul, a wild-eyed, English hippie raved about two things: his overland trip to India and the beautiful ladies of Copenhagen. My travel companion was afraid to cross the Bosphorous, but he was up to check out the action in Denmark. You make decisions like that when you are seventeen.

Despite all the hoopla, I found it frustratingly hard to get laid in this supposed den of iniquity and easy ladies. Perhaps my youth betrayed me... but, tough sledding—tough, tough sledding.

My musical passion then was the jazz of **John Coltrane, Archie Shepp, Ornette Coleman, Roland Kirk** and the like. I used to hit the London jazz spots, like **Ronnie Scott's**, hard—and followed the same program in Copenhagen.

A radiant, fresh-faced blonde showed up also almost every night at the **Jazzhus Montmartre**, my favorite hangout. I did my best to entice her into something more, but it was not to be...

The closest it ever got was a visit to my apartment the night before I left for London. Her boyfriend was away in Yugoslavia. I sensed an opportunity. We lay in bed staring at each other, holding each other, but that was all she wrote...

Seven years later, in 1975, I was doggedly pursuing enlightenment at the **Bhagwan Rajneesh** ashram in Poona, India. I had rented a spacious apartment nearby. In the Tai Chi class, a red-haired Danish lady was a dedicated co-student. Her girlfriend was sharing my apartment. She asked me if the Danish lady could move in to the vacant room. Sure...

Six months later, Danish and I were sitting opposite each other in the kitchen, sharing a juice. Something jogged in me. I looked at her intently then asked, "Do you have a sister—and is your dad a butcher?"

The veils dropped and we recognized each other. It was my friend from the Jazzhus Monmartre.

CHAPTER 4

Sexcapades

How to Survive Being Raped by a Beatnik

When you are sixteen years old and hanging out at clubs like **UFO,** on 31 Tottenham Court Road, London—to watch the house bands **Pink Floyd** and **The Soft Machine**—you can end up the night in some surprising places…

One night, a short, bearded beatnik in his forties slunk up and started to chat in a natural, easy, humorous way. I went along with his banter. "Know where I could score some hash?" I asked him. He suggested we try another club I liked to visit, **The Roaring Twenties**, on 50 Carnaby Street. Lots of West Indians and Africans there and great music. Just had to stay out of the random knife fight, punch up or half-hearted police raid…

The built West Indian gentleman who sold us the hunk of hash came back with us to the beatnik's squalid basement flat. He rolled up a massive splif and we started passing it around.

I got in over my head, started to feel nauseous and terribly stoned—told the two I needed to lie down on the ratty couch. I heard an ominous question from the West Indian: "Who's going to be the bigger beast?" Thankfully the beatnik pressed his prior claim and the dealer took off.

Next thing I knew, the beatnik was squirming around on top of me. I barfed all over the floor. While Scruffman cleaned it up, I crawled into the middle of his carpet.

But the vomiting was no deterrent. Back on top of me he went, begging me to do him… somehow, he got his foul-tasting mouth on mine, before I could twist away. I threw up again. When he ran to mop up a second time, I bolted out and into the street, followed by forlorn cries of "Come back, come back!"

This little escapade had some dramatic consequences. Shortly after, I came down with raging gingivitis—and eventually had to have my gums cut back.

JACKIE BE GOOD

Sitting in the backroom of **Max's Kansas City** with **Taylor Mead** one night, **Jackie Curtis** flounced up and sat beside me. Jackie had written an off-off-Broadway play in which she also starred. She was fresh from the show, in full dress costume, with silver glitter on her rouged cheeks.

"Jackie, this is John" offered Taylor with his sly grin. "Hello, John". Jackie gazed at me—as her hand slid to my groin and started stroking my junk. I got hard. With my hardness in complete control of my brain, I blurted "Let's go to your place." Jackie pulled back, startled. A casual shock-tease-come-on—met with an offer.

We headed out and jumped into a Yellow. In the back seat, I stared at Jackie's profile. In the harshest of harsh late-night street lighting, coarse man-stubble showed through Jackie's make up. Damn, I was in some pickle of my own making... I had zero interest in sex with any kind of male—and most certainly not with this thick-set, hairy guy.

But the trigger was pulled and we headed uptown to the apartment Jackie shared with a beautiful Indian actress. Could there be a last-moment switch here? Wasn't going to happen.

Jackie was good-natured and kind. She took my inability to get properly aroused in stride. We parted on friendly enough terms...

Whenever I hear that **Walk on the Wild Side** line "Jackie thought she was James Dean for a day", I remember this interlude.

YOU WANT BEAUTIFUL LADY COME?

The Chinese authorities send mixed messages about sex work. Almost every spa and massage place seems to offer more than just therapeutic services. It is prevalent enough that you might assume it was legal. It's not. The powers appear to let things ride, then every now and then stomp down hard. Sometimes very hard: one gentleman recently got sentenced to death for running a prostitution ring in Shenzhen...

On one of my first visits to China, I got my introduction to one such set up.

The **Sino Swiss Hotel Beijing Airport** looked not too bad on the web. But the reality was more than a little sketchy…

I had some time to kill in the morning, so decided to check out the hotel spa. Now, the spa was located straight off the main lobby through a wide-open passage way. No doors.

The massage table was behind a kind of hospital screen. There was draping, but the public could waltz right in, any time they cared to…

The massage was terrific. Solid Tui-na. But near the end, the solid Tui-na started to morph into some subtle, carressive finger-tip work. She was signaling a fresh agenda.

The therapist lent over my face and whispered: "You want beautiful lady come now, give you special massage?"

Well, there is a time and a place for all kinds of hanky panky, right?

But in broad, bright daylight, in plain view to the curious and in a semi-clinical setting—nah, I think I'll pass, thanks…

Not With the Driver, Honey

In desperate days, struggling to get Dragon Door airborne, I took part-time work as a limo driver.

I saw some things… and here's a choice example:

In the glow of a summer's evening, I picked up a 3M engineer and his speech-pathologist wife. The engineer had a snickering laugh that issued from him in stuttered bursts of self-involvement. The lady was all woman—luscious and exuding sensuality.

We headed to Minneapolis and picked up an elegant couple—a suave African American doctor and his sweet-faced, blonde partner. Off to dinner after a ride around the lake… through the divider I heard furtive rustlings, grunts and giggles. Sexual scents wafted through the cracks. Pulling open the door at the restaurant, the blonde was embarrassed and red-faced as she adjusted her clothing.

On the way to **Glam Slam**, the divider slid down and half of the speech pathologist pushed herself through the gap… "I love you!" she cried, turning into me. "Not with the driver!" shouted her husband, as he yanked her back into the melee behind.

Waiting, as limo drivers wait so much… then 3M came scuttling out of the club and asked me to drive him, alone, to a nearby strip club. After a quickie at the strip joint, we bolted back to the oblivious trio at Glam Slam…

"I'm a pervert!" he whispered to me with a cackle and gleeful wink when we parted at the end of the night.

IS THIS A DATE?

The Americans invented "dating"—although they are always startled when I tell them so...

It all began with the rise of the automobile in the United States. For the first time, young couples could go out by themselves, unchaperoned, in a car—and have their way with each other: The Date. No such luck for almost all English and Europeans. Relatively car-less and overcrowded, we went out in gangs and mobs, whatever the final intention might be... A generalization, but you get my drift.

When I first moved to Minnesota in 1985, I was constantly thrown by the frequent references to "dating". Was this a straight euphemism for sex? Or something more general? Depended on the person and the situation, it appeared.

I was interested in this one lady and invited her to dinner and a movie. As we drove to the movie, she asked me hesitatingly, "Is this a date?" I was kinda floored... just mumbled something noncommittal back at her.

The conversation turned to her recent divorce. She had left her husband for another person. When I asked who the new guy had been, she clarified that it was a woman—which explained the hesitant question about the date...

We did still end in bed—for a little bit. After a while of gentle caressing and closeness, she looked at me, "John, you appeal to the five percent of me that is attracted to men…"

CHAPTER 5

Tall Tales

WHEN MY DAD TORPEDOED THE BISMARCK

ON MAY 26TH, 1941, MY dad took off from the ***Ark Royal*** aircraft carrier in a Faery Swordfish. His mission: torpedo and sink the Nazi battleship ***Bismarck***.

Now imagine: you are flying an ancient bi-plane toward one full side of Germany's most powerful warship. Every gun is blazing away at you. You skim the waves, approaching at approximately 120 mph…

The Swordfish suddenly lightens as the torpedo releases. You rear up and bank away…

And you make it—mostly because your plane flew too slow and low for the gunners' fire-control predictors to nail you.

Safely out of range, you turn to give your rear gunner a smiling thumbs-up. Neither the smile nor the thumbs-up are returned. The poor blighter has lost his head—shot off as the plane banked away…

I told this story many times to my children. A hero tale, lionizing their grandpa.

But the story is not exactly accurate. Yes, my dad flew Faery Swordfish torpedo bombers in the Second World War. Yes, the Bismarck was crippled by such an attack on May 26th, 1941.

But he did not participate in this battle. At all…

I caught flak from my kids—in particular, my son—for having made up this tale… they feel betrayed, somehow.

But I don't regret the telling of it. It's an embellishment, a wish fulfillment and a measure of how I really saw my dad…

DEATH BY CROCODILE

The red clay roads in the fifties in Sierra Leone would often lead down to a swollen river with no bridge.

Two chains span the river. The chains run either side of a ferry of pontoons, empty gasoline drums and wooden planks. The ferrymen yank on the chains to pull the load across.

In 1957, my parents, my brother and I were waiting to cross by such a ferry. But first an ancient mammy wagon teetered onto the planks, stuffed with squawking chickens, ladies in a riot of brightly-colored clothing, half-naked, squalling kids…

Downstream were some rocks and rapids with crocodiles basking nearby on the muddy banks…

A snapping sound—like a gunshot. Cries of alarm. One of the chains had broken. The ferry swung around and started to tilt over. A massive crashing and screaming—the hugely over-burdened mammy wagon had toppled over, spraying its load into the river.

The force of the rapids sucked the mammies and their kids down toward the waiting rocks...

I gazed toward the muddy banks: the crocodiles had disappeared... but wait, there they were, their snouts and eyes and spiny backs gliding toward the oncoming gift of fresh flesh...

Many drowned that day and some were eaten, we later learned.

Shaken, we climbed back into the dusty Land Rover and beat our retreat.

This is another tale told as entertainment for my kids, weaving in some truths with some blatant embellishments.

Everything is true in this story until the point at which the fictionalizer asks the question: "What if one of those chains broke in mid-stream?"

CHAPTER 6

Accidents Happen

HIT-AND-RUN AT THE CARIBOU DRIVE-THRU

ON AN EASTER SUNDAY, I was idling at a Caribou Coffee drive thru, waiting on my triple espresso. Crunch! I was jolted forward in my seat. A gray SUV had banged into my rear…

I slid out of my Chrysler 300, noted the sizable dent in my rear fender and signaled the SVU's driver. The fifty-something church lady rolled down her window about one third of the way.

"Let's pull over into the parking lot to exchange information," I said.

"Why? There is no damage" she replied.

"There most definitely is—look—so let's pull over"

I got my espresso and pulled into the lot.

Boom: she bolted, like a bat from the belfry…

Perhaps no insurance? But stupid really—she was risking a year in prison if we had tracked her down.

Failed to catch her plates, however. And no CCTV. The lady escaped scot-free.

The sleezoid's final gift to me: $2,300 in repairs, a banged-up neck—and a whole bunch of hate…

IT HURTS TO BE DOUBLE REAR-ENDED

Leaving Portland Airport in a rental to attend a five-day shamanic qigong retreat on the Oregon coast with **Master Wu**. Paused at a stoplight.

The rental lurches, my head snaps back. A rust-red truck has smashed into the back of us… I turn my head to see the truck reverse away. Then, with my neck still twisted round, I watch as the truck careens forward and crashes into my rear a second time.

Let me tell you: it hurts to be rear-ended. And it hurts a hell of a lot more when your neck is twisted sideways…

The truck reverses a second time. Two minutes pass. The truck is idling, coughing up a lung…

I choose to jump out and walk back to the truck. Who is this—and why me?

A weather-beaten man in his seventies is mortified and apologetic. He's a recovering cancer patient. Lost control of his foot on the pedal. Twice…

Bizarre enough to believe.

I wished him well and went on my way.

CHAPTER 7

Physical Foolishness

THE TURKISH ARMY TRUCK

DRIVING THROUGH TURKEY IN 1969 had its own set of traffic-related challenges. A round-about might as well have had signs that said: "Direction Optional" and "Make Way If You Feel Like It." Once, laboring up a steep hill near Ankara, I had to veer entirely off the road—because three battered trucks had just rolled over the brow of the hill, abreast…

But our experience with a Turkish Army troop transport near Mount Ararat took the cake…

The transport lumbered along in the middle of the road forever and a day, making it impossible to pass. Cheerful soldiers waved at us through the rear canvas flapping in the wind…

Suddenly, the truck switched to the wrong side of the road— and stayed there.

Okay…

I gunned our pathetic excuse of an engine and started to overtake the truck.

Which is what they were waiting for…

We were almost past them when the driver swerved to hit us and caught our back. We half-tailed toward the ditch, but our speed was just enough—and we fish-tailed to safety ahead of the truck.

We looked back at the driver and his mate: they were splitting their sides.

Nice set up guys…

How to Finger Death While Windsurfing in a Speedo

Windsurfing without a wetsuit on a windy day off the coast of Dinard, Brittany. Skinny guy, with just a Speedo between him and the elements. A chop to the ocean. A bone-chilling cold…

I am at best a poorish windsurfer, with scant skills and not much nautical sense to back it up. So, when the tides and the sudden gusts conspired to strand me far from the rocky shore, I ended up dismasting, lying on the board and paddling.

I am not sure how many shiver-shaken hours I spent out there… Long enough…

About two weeks later in Minnesota, I developed a feeling of tightness and constriction on the left side of my chest. I labored to breathe without pain. When I started to also heat up and my temperature blew past 103, I headed to urgent care.

The physician did her best to hide her alarm. Glad I couldn't read her mind…

They stuck me in the back with a massive syringe—and siphoned out a pint or so of yellow fluid. Pleural effusion, they called it.

The medical staff rescued me from the immediate crisis. However, they had no idea about what may have caused the condition—or what to do to prevent it in the future.

My acupuncturist, **Chris Hafner**, was entirely unsurprised. "A classic case of wind invasion!" he observed. Chris treated me with needles, herbs—advised including pork chops, mushrooms, green beans and astragalus in my diet.

The protocols worked. The condition subsided and never returned.

East and West had gang-tackled me back to health...

HERE, SMOKE THIS OIL

In 1973, a friend of mine smuggled hash oil back from Nepal in film cans. I got into the prolonged and persistent habit of drinking that godly goo—mixed into a cocktail with Cointreau.

Or, I would stick a cig into a bottle of the black tar and fire that up...

Or, I would soak tobacco in a hash oil solution, bake it in the oven, then roll up spliffs from the proceeds…

While the subsequent zone out was perfect for listening to Dub Reggae or endless repetitions of **Catch a Fire**, it did zippo for my work and social life. I became increasingly isolated in my own befuddled reveries. Hovering above my body, I feared danger behind every corner…

The International Festival of Independent Avant-Garde Film in September included a party for all the film makers—a wild bunch, to put it mildly. I brought a heavily-laced Cointreau bottle to the gathering and offered free slugs to all comers. As a result, the party disintegrated into madness and mayhem…

The principal host, **Annabel Nicholson**, was infuriated and felt that I had destroyed the party, accusing me of a "Fascist" act…

I hosted my own party for the film makers a couple of days later. The angry and resentful stayed away out of protest—but there were plenty of hopefuls to take up the slack…

Suck My Gasoline

I forget her name—and let's keep it that way. Met her around '69 in London. She was an American living in Paris. We were both broke—and somewhere and somehow, I agreed to a wild scheme of hers to defraud her insurance company...

The plot was this: we would drive from Paris to Turin, Italy. Spend the night and drive back. She would report that a bunch of her stuff was stolen from her car in Turin. We would split the final take 50/50.

There was a hitch: we had no gas money for the trip.

I agreed to syphon the gas we needed, all the way to and from...

Now, prolonged sucking of gasoline is probably not good for your health... And it also makes you high as a kite in a gale...

Case in point: In Nice, at 2 in the morning, we found ourselves jammed between two vehicles on a side street. We bumped forward and ended up hooked to the front vehicle's rear fender. No worries. We accelerated backwards—and the rear fender came ripping off with an immense metallic screeching noise. We high-tailed it out of there and in our frenzy, came darn close to driving straight into the ocean...

Turin was not good to me. The lady at the cheapo hotel was outraged at the idea of the two of us un-marrieds taking a room together. I slept fitfully in the car that night, surrounded by reeking gas cans.

My final pay off for this escapade was surely the hardest-earned money I ever made.

SHIT, BUT BEAUTIFULLY COOKED

My dad was on an extended sailing trip with some mates. They shanghaied Henry into being the galley slave. The claim was that he was such a damn fine chef, it would be a crime against the profession for anybody else to be cooking up the grub.

Henry put up this nonsense for a few days, then he flipped his lid…

After retrieving the contents of his bowels, he prepared my dad and his mates a special meal…

On deck, the plates were served out. Jacques was ahead of the game and forked in a mouthful of the main dish…

Jacques looked thoughtful for a moment then lent over the side and spat the half-masticated, fried turd into the unsuspecting ocean waves.

"Shit," said Jacques, "but beautifully cooked."

This apocryphal story stayed with me into my Cambridge days and inspired me to cook a special dinner of shit burgers for two of my Eng. Lit. buddies. I fried up my shit in patties—liberally spiced with Garam Masala—then presented the carefully-garnished burgers on my best china.

My mates had done me no wrong, so fair's fair, I waited until Chris and Fred had a piece each poised at their lips before screaming "Stop!"

Being very stoned-out at the same time, they took the prank in good stride—and to the best of my knowledge there was never any pay back…

THE EXPLODING EYEBALL

In 2012, **At Bill** and **Allison Helm's** *Taoist Sanctuary* in San Diego, I took **Chen Style Cannon Fist** from Grandmaster **Chen Xiaoxing**. Cannon Fist is a very athletic form, with rapid, explosive strikes—and one spectacular, 360-degree "jump and pound" move. Out of a desire to burn that move in—and to impress Chen Xiaoxing with my dedication—I pounded away at that one technique with maniacal intensity and foolish frequency.

I was 63 at the time. I have some toughness, but it was senseless to put my ravaged right knee through that extended plyometric pounding. However, there was a far more significant age-related vulnerability lurking in the shadows…

When I woke up the next morning, I could barely see out of my left eye. A dirty, gray mist floated and squiggled across my retina.

Was I about to go blind in one eye? Or both eyes?

I rushed to the eye specialist. "Nothing I can do for you," he said. "You have floaters. They may stay, but if you are lucky they will just subside over time."

Thanks doc!

Online research: particles of collagen and hyaluronic acid had broken loose within the eyeball—an age-related vulnerability that doesn't appreciate repetitive shocks and jolts. The good news was that the jumping and pounding hadn't resulted in a retinal tear—which could, indeed, have led to possible vision loss.

The apparent floaters remained for longer than I liked, to the point that I considered a radical laser treatment. The physician I eventually visited told me that what had really happened was some micro-bleeding within the eyeball—and that I was experiencing the visual effects of that blood swirling around. Nice. He declined to operate, telling me the condition would slowly disappear, which it did.

The wakeup call for me was to recalibrate my fitness-practice goals. Why was I doing what I was doing? What was the risk-reward ratio in my practice? More and more, for me, the ratio is skewed toward health and longevity. I can satisfy my sense of self-worth in many more effective ways than by leaping up and down on hard floors to impress my teacher...

CHAPTER 8

Travel Tales

Bugging Out with the Criminally Insane

I don't advise getting bombed out of your mind in the number one maximum security prison for the criminally insane in the United States.

In 1970, underground filmmaker John Schofill had noted a phallic water tower he wanted to capture for his movie. He parked nearby and started prepping his Ariflex. I figured I might as well pick up a few frames myself with by 16mm Bolex.

I was clipping away at the big phallus, when a police jeep screeched to a halt next to me. "You're under arrest. You're photographing on state property." Inviting me to join them in their jeep, we headed over to pick up Mr. John and his Ari…

Noting the barbed wire and gun towers, we were led inside the building. Electronic doors and men in white coats…

We were told we were in the number one prison for the criminally insane in the US. The guards figured we were part of some radical group like SDS, making an anti-establishment documentary. They grilled us on who we were and what we were up to.

John was not being very communicative. His eyes were bugging out of his head and he kept staring at me in a creepy kind of way. What I didn't know until later was that he was stoned out of his gourd… We had had a stash of mushrooms in the car—and he ate all of them when he saw the police jeep approaching.

They kept us for around four hours while they checked me out with the British Embassy and checked John out with the Chicago Art Institute, where he was supposedly teaching film.

Once we checked out clean, the guards became very amiable indeed. The warden's parting, genial offer: "Hey, if you ever want to come back and make a film here, we'll see what we can do for you…"

CAN I KILL YOU WITH THIS PEN?

In 1969, on a college vacation, I drove a VW Bus from London to Benares, India and back. Two ladies, myself and two guys. We sallied through Turkey, Iran, Afghanistan, Pakistan—on the hippy trail of the times…

One of my Cambridge mates on the trip, **Mali Mustapha**, was a Tanzanian of Pakistani origin. His uncle was a captain in the Pakistan Air Force. We stayed with the uncle in Peshawar, on the edge of the Khyber Pass.

The Captain had bombed a local tribal chief's village some time back. They'd met later at a party and became best of friends…

"I bombed your village, haha!"

"You bombed my village, I love you, haha!"

The Chief had his own private arms factory up in the mountains. He invited the five of us to check out his village and stash of weapons.

The factory was not much more than a series of open, wooden sheds, really. But there they were, churning out rifles and pistols of every kind and make...

The Chief gave me a gift of a metal fountain pen that fired a .22 bullet when you pulled back and released its pocket clip. Smirking, he unscrewed the end of the pen, aimed at the sky— and popped a cap.

My most treasured souvenir from the whole trip...

RIFLES AT THE BORDER

The VW Bus, painted with red Sanskrit mantras, putters up to English Customs after disgorging from the ferry.

Stuffed in the back: loot from the overland trip to India. Wolf skins, Afghan jackets, Lee Enfield rifles, ancient temple artifacts, flamboyant hippie clothing, strings of big-beaded malas, rugs—oh and a bunch of hash stashed in a large calor gas container...

Hash? Now, that was not very sensible of us—as we drove that hash with us back through Afghanistan, Iran and Turkey. None of these countries known for the niceness of their prisons…

"Anything to declare?" asked Customs Guy.

"Yes," I replied. "Two rifles."

"Two rifles!" He was confounded.

I handed the Enfields over for inspection. Supposedly they had been captured or stolen from the British Army, at some point, in Afghanistan.

Customs Guy scoffed. "No problem, these are not rifles! If they had been, we would have had to confiscate them."

Turns out, these guns were ancient enough that their barrels had no rifling. So, we were off the hook…

The officer was sufficiently thrown by the Lee Enfields, to not even ask what else we might be carrying—or to carry out any kind of search. He didn't even look at our passports to see where we had come from—or care apparently.

We all had a good laugh of relief, once safely out of his range…

GO BACK TO YOUR ROOM, YOU ARE UNDER INVESTIGATION

The Shangri La Hotel, Qingdao, China, 2009. Here to visit kettlebell factories. Time for breakfast before meeting up with my Chinese contacts. 7:30am, I step out of the elevator…

Seven men in black block my way. A lady approaches at a cautious distance and tells me: "Go back to your room. You are under investigation." A calmness washes through me.

No one joins me in the elevator.

Inside my room, I hear a rustling outside the door. Peer through the peephole. Yellow crime tape crisscrosses the corridor in front. I retreat.

The bell buzzes. I open. Two men in Hazmat suits enter. "Relax," says one of them. His eyes smile at me.

No sweat, I am being detained by the Chinese Government for the next full week…

Turns out that a passenger on my flight from Narita has come down with Swine Flu (which they now estimate killed around 284,000 people worldwide that year). The government has tracked down every person on my flight for isolation and observation.

The smiling CDC men in the Hazmat suits fitted me out in a similar rig. My entire belongings got bagged up in heavy plastic. The CDC escorted me into the bowels of the hotel, as anxious staff peered around the corners… Then up to a large, isolated suite.

The mood remained light-hearted. I successfully persuaded one of the gentlemen to photograph me in Tai Chi poses while in my Hazmat—perfect for social media…

Living in the lap of luxury at the expense of the Chinese Government was a fair trade for the loss of my freedom for a week.

I coughed one time. The phone rang. "You cough, take temperature now."

Another day, I wasn't feeling hungry and didn't eat my lunch. The phone rang. "You don't eat lunch. Why?"

They released me with kindness on the seventh day and I hooked back up with my Chinese kettlebell colleagues.

You Very Strong. Why?

I love bodywork of all kinds. I particularly love Chinese bodywork—Tui Na, foot massage, you name it. When I am in China I get a massage every day—the price is right, the skill-level is out of sight and the experience is almost always fantastic. I leave feeling relaxed and energized.

The English language skills of the Chinese massage therapists can be quite limited—and my own Chinese a joke. Our communications become a mixture of grunts, hand signals, smiles, grimaces, laughter, groans and the occasional cryptic comment.

My favorite quote of all time was in Qingdao. After beating on me for 90 minutes, my Chinese therapist exclaimed "You very strong!" Then she paused, looked puzzled and asked: "Why?"

Being doped up on a 90-minute proprioceptive-neuro-buzz, I failed to provide a coherent answer. But the incident dramatizes the fact that you can't take your own drive for physical cultivation for granted. And for many people—even skilled bodyworkers—it's apparently a mystery that you have a strong body at all. Or why you bother…

Part of the answer lies, of course, in Michelangelo's comment "If people knew how hard I worked to gain my mastery, it wouldn't seem so wonderful at all."

The obese monstrosities waddling around Walmart didn't drop from the sky that way. They slobbed themselves into those globs of egregious fat. Those of us who choose to defy entropy—and cultivate ourselves as physical specimens—work to earn our bodies…

So: Why be strong? For hundreds of reasons, really—most of them functional. But for now, let's answer in terms of a species-basic, primal reality: body-pride and self-pride.

We are animals that are blessed with the uncanny ability to transform ourselves physically—both in function and form. Diligent work physically transforms you mentally and spiritually—while molding you into a more handsome/beautiful specimen.

You only have this one body in this life—and the older you get the more you appreciate that.

RECKLESS IN GIZA

In 1975, I bought a ticket from London to Bombay on Egypt Air, on my way to the **Bhagwan Rajneesh** ashram in Poona, India. We stopped for the night in Cairo…

Sleepless in my empty hotel room, I watched the full moon pouring through the broken window panes. It hit me: why not head out to the Great Pyramid of Giza nearby, climb to the top of it and meditate as the sun rose to flood me with light? A transcendental experience if ever there was one to be had…

Before dawn broke, I was out by the Great Pyramid and looking for a way to climb up…

A raggedy, emaciated creature limped up to me. "You cannot climb the pyramid, it is forbidden!" He paused, "But for one pound, I show you secret way…"

Up he scampered, with me in tow. We reached the top with perfect timing, just before the sun was about to rise. I crossed my legs into a full lotus, closed my eyes and readied myself for my profound mystical moment.

There was a tug on my sleeve and a hiss from my guide. "You want souvenir from Egypt?" I looked round. He was pointing at his bulging crotch.

I clambered back down the pyramid, pursued by urgent cries…

Fortunately, a young Scandinavian lady appeared on top of a sand dune and my guide ran toward her, for the next scam of the day. I was freed up to be alone with the Great Sphinx in the still early dawn…

PAN-FRIED WASPS ON THE HOLY MOUNTAIN

The most special meal I have eaten in my life was in the valley of a Taoist holy mountain. Mt. Laoshan was a dreamscape of phallic rocks, labial crevices, glittering streams, serene pools and wind-brushed trees. A classic painting sprung to life…

My Chinese hosts and I hiked on the magical tracks for hours of quiet ecstasy. Late in the golden afternoon, we sat satisfied at a restaurant serving specialties from the mountain. The deepest, most yellow of eggs, the richest and most succulent of greens, mysterious mushrooms with rumored healing powers…

But the greatest delicacy was the pan-fried wasps. You just had to get over those twin demon eyes staring out at you from the plate—and the intact sting in the tail…

Crunching down on those critters provoked as rich a taste-explosion in my watering mouth as I could possibly have ever hoped for…

BORDEAUX REDS IN RIOT

In 1973, I presented a film of mine at an independent film festival in Bordeaux. My invitation had been greased by the vampire-cloaked Belgian eccentric **Roland Lethem**.

My film caused a riot. Punch-ups flared in the audience. Roland and I barricaded ourselves in the projection booth as furious patrons thumped on the door, wanting to tear the film off its spools. Glassy, swollen-faced, bearded types gesticulated and brandished cardboard between the light beams and the screen.

At the end of the debacle, I braved the crowd. One young gentleman in particular tossed insults in my direction. The gist was that my abstract structuralism was a form of "aristocratic elitism"—a whorish insult to the proletarian sensibility.

This was a period of leftist fervor in independent film circles— where wonky camera shots of angry workers waving fists in front of padlocked factory gates was the way to go… Agitprop.

Despite all the posturing and fist waving, nobody physically attacked me. I left the auditorium intact.

The next evening, I boarded a sleeper for Paris. The compartment door slid open and in walked my Insulter from the riot. Alone without his compadres, he looked sheepish and gave me an awkward nod.

We traveled together to Paris without exchanging a word…

Life Is Short—Stay Away from It

Back in the day, I was waiting inside a local Caribou to pick up my triple espresso. This frumpy, plump lady bloused into the shop and closed on the barista. She let out a sudden squawk: "Life is short, stay away from it!"

She had misread the Caribou slogan: "Life is short. Stay awake for it!"

They served her anyway…

This vignette has lodged in my mind ever since. You could riff for hours on the philosophical nuances of fleeing from life vs. engaging life full tilt.

CHAPTER 9

Death and Dying

He Shot Himself for Thinking Too Much

Julian was a doctoral student in Moral Sciences at Cambridge. I met him in the street one day and after some discussion invited him to take an empty room in the house I was renting. He accepted.

Julian told me later that he had been on his way to buy a shotgun to blow his brains out. He decided to give life one more chance on receiving my invitation. But it turned out to be just a temporary stay of execution…

My philosopher friend also confessed to having murdered a tramp late one night on a Cambridge commons. I had little reason to doubt the sincerity of his confession, which was delivered with barely a hint of emotion.

Julian was one tortured cat. Also, one of the most brilliant minds I've ever met. His was a terrifying inquiry into the nature and meaning of life that brooked no quarter. He sought out the greatest philosophers of his generation—in person—attempting to solve the mysteries of the universe. With no joy.

It was impossible to hold a superficial conversation with Julian. The casual banter that lubricates relationships would devolve in a heartbeat into an agonizing analysis of some arcane puzzle with no foreseeable solution.

Julian thought himself to death. I watched his thinking process spiral him up his ass so deep there was eventually no way to back out.

So, one day, my roommate **Gautaum Tendulkar** found Julian's brains splashed across the back wall and ceiling of his upstairs room. Another roommate, **Roger Whitney**, picked up scraps of messages by Julian, discarded carefully around the garden—a final set of hieroglyphic pleas for connection and recognition of his pain…

THE DOG AND THE DOCTOR'S DAUGHTER

This dog killed my first girlfriend—she was five and I was six…

Suzie came in screaming to her dad, the mining camp doctor, a bite wound on her arm. A stray hound had given her a nip—then skulked off into the bush, never to be found.

In Sierra Leone rabies ran rampant in the mangy curs who infested the district. No such thing as a safe dog, a nice dog.

In the fifties, it took several horse needles of vaccine into the stomach to save the victim of an attack. For small children, the effects of the injections could be traumatic, even fatal. The dad decided to wait a while, in the hope his daughter was not infected. She appeared to be ok, so he held off on the vaccine.

Several weeks later, Suzie suddenly collapsed, foaming at the mouth. Too late for help, she died in agony…

My parents shielded us from the details of Suzie's death. But they doubled down on their warnings about the dangers of dogs. To this day, any approaching dog puts me on initial guard…

When I finally got told the full story, it always seemed too bad to be true. How could the doctor have risked his daughter's life in such a manner? I quizzed my dad, not long before he died, about this tale. Had I heard it wrong? Had memory played tricks on me? Was I making things up?

Nope, was my dad's reply. It really did happen that way…

DEATH OF THE MOTHER

A few years before she did die, my mother said to me, "Don't cry for us when we die. We've had a wonderful life." Spoken with a direct certainty. I thought at the time: "I wish I could end my days with that kind of a statement, but there's no way I can wrap 'wonderful' around the turbulence of my past."

And I was to learn soon enough that the tears would flow freely—the loss all mine, tinged with the regrets of missed opportunities for connection and intimacy.

I got the news from my Dad in England that my mother was dying and to fly over right away.

I was not prepared for what I would find with her as she lay on her death bed in the hospital.

Walking through the door, I saw my mother looking about one hundred years older than when I'd seen her about a month before.

My mother opened her eyes and her face transformed into a local of utter radiant joy and love—no filter, just the purity of it. I burst into a torrent of tears that didn't let up for my whole visit.

It was the most transcendent experience of my life.

Clutching her wafer-thin hand, the feeling of loss and bereavement consumed me as nothing has ever done—and ever will…

My mother's last words to me, delivered with a flood of love and the clearest, happiest, most fulfilled eyes:

"You know who to say goodbye to…"

Only in her death, did I come to love my mother in the fullness of my heart—and mourn her every day since… Only in her death.

DEATH OF THE FATHER

My dad died on Thursday November 1st, 2012, a few months after my mother. I missed his actual death by a couple of days, which is how I feel he wanted it…

The last weekend of my father's life, Andrea and I were in the UK for an RKC kettlebell certification. The workshop was in Bury St Edmunds and we planned to visit him briefly afterwards, before flying back to the US on the Tuesday.

That Saturday, on an errand, I ended up by error on a back road of the University of Suffolk. Ahead, I saw a smallish cylinder sticking slightly out of the ground. I figured it was some kind of traffic device that had been deactivated…

Soldier on, right? I figured I would just drive over the Thing…

As my brand-new Passat rental passed over the Thing, there was a massive explosion and the car ground to a halt.

Turns out I was the victim of an infernal British invention: the Bollard. The Thing had totaled the vehicle, entirely wrecking the engine—which was exactly what it was designed to do. How on earth the British public accept this kind of viciousness still boggles my mind.

"Well, bollocks to you, Bollard!" I spent several hours getting rescued and towed back to Heathrow Airport, where I was given a replacement rental without—mercifully—being hit with some egregious penalty for willful foolishness.

On the Sunday evening, we made it to my dad's apartment. He was clearly in very bad shape and not wanting to engage us long. We fed him some orange juice and promised to see him next morning, before we headed back to the States.

Monday around 11am we showed up. He was sitting up on his pillows, wearing light-gold pajamas—and greeted us with "Oh, No!" Distressed to have any company at all. We said our goodbyes quickly.

At the doorway, I heard his last words, delivered with one raised fist: "I'm not going out on you!"

We got the call on Thursday. He had died in peace that afternoon.

And dad, you never did go out on me…

Why I Ate My Dad

I ate my father after he died. Here's why…

At my dad's request, my brother Peter and I met in Dinard, Brittany to pour his ashes over the ocean, where he had sailed from childhood into his late seventies.

We rented the same kind of inflatable attack-boat favored by the SEALs. Our pilot turned out to be a sun-damaged, French ex-Special Forces operative.

Unfortunately, the weather on the chosen day was dreadful. Serious white caps and a howling wind. We attempted to persist and beat out into the raging waves. It was just ridiculous… So much for the leisurely, thoughtful, soulful remembrance planned…

Plan B was to hightail it into the bay beneath the chateau where my parents had lived for a while. At least we could imagine my ghostly father staring down on us from the rocky heights, as we released his ashes back into his beloved ocean…

As my brother poured the ashes into the sea, a sudden gust blew the fine dust of my dad into my eyes—coated my face with his gray, powdery remains…

We bobbed on the wild water, first fighting, then yielding to the rising and the falling and the breaking and the pitching and the spraying…

Hunkered down in the dingy, we shared a rich Breton picnic of meats and cheeses with our Spec Ops man, then called it a day.

That evening, my brother gave me a small metal container with a half-ounce or so of the ashes, which I brought back with me to Minnesota.

I'm not sure how I arrived at the thought, but:

I decided to eat some of my father's ashes. Some kind of atavistic impulse to absorb his essence. It felt like a final, sacred homage—but somehow also very forbidden, very taboo...

I chose a Sri Lankan restaurant in Minneapolis, **The Dancing Ganesh**. I ordered up one of their most fiery curries. Sprinkled a little of my dad into the mix—and ate him...

The act was very special—mystical really. A way of taking his being into me in the most intimate manner possible. An act of love.

I have placed the rest of his ashes in a drawer beneath my favorite Buddha...

71315732R00053

Made in the USA
Columbia, SC
24 May 2017